From Fear to Fortune

Turning AI Chaos into Personal and Business Prosperity

Taylor Royce

Copyright © 2024 Taylor Royce

All rights reserved.

DEDICATION

To those who have the fortitude and curiosity to face the future. This book is devoted to the visionaries, dreamers, and inventors who work to use technology for the benefit of society. I hope that perseverance, ingenuity, and a resolute dedication to advancement will steer your path. Let's work together to turn obstacles into opportunities and create a better future.

CONTENTS

ACKNOWLEDGMENTS 1

CHAPTER 1 1

Getting to Know AI Fear 1

   1.1 AI's Ascent and Effects 1

   1.2 The Impact of AI Disruption on the Mind 3

   1.3 The Surprisingly High Rate of AI Anxiety 5

CHAPTER 2 9

How Much It Costs to Avoid AI 9

   2.1 Lost Chances in Careers and Business 9

   2.2 The Individual Cost of Avoiding AI 12

   2.3 How Failure to Understand AI Will Affect Success in the Future. 15

CHAPTER 3 20

Converting Fear into Inquisitiveness 20

   3.1 Recasting the Story of AI 20

   3.2 How to Develop a Growth Mentality in the Age of AI 23

   3.3 AI Success Story Case Studies 27

CHAPTER 4 31

Using AI as a Tool for Personal Development 31

   4.1 AI and Personal Development 31

   4.2 AI in Wellness and Health 35

   4.3 Harmonizing AI and Individual Satisfaction 38

CHAPTER 5 42

Using AI to Grow Your Company 42

    5.1 Using AI to Make Strategic Decisions..42

    5.2 Using AI to Simplify Operations..45

    5.3 Using AI to Improve Customer Experience...................................48

CHAPTER 6...**53**

Breaking Down Business Barriers to AI Adoption........................ **53**

    6.1 Recognizing Typical Obstacles to AI Adoption............................ 54

    6.2 Creating a Team Prepared for AI.. 57

    6.3 Leadership's Significance in AI Integration..................................60

CHAPTER 7...**64**

Ethical AI: Aligning Technology with Values E..............................**64**

    7.1 Comprehending AI's Ethical Difficulties..64

    7.2 Making Responsible Use of AI in Your Company........................ 68

    7.3 Accountability's Function in AI-Powered Decision Making.......... 72

CHAPTER 8...**77**

Succeeding with AI Without Compromise on Well-Being...................**77**

    8.1 Combining AI with a Well-Being Lifestyle......................................77

    8.2 AI Time Management Tools for Individuals..................................80

    8.3 The Value of Human Relationships in an AI Age.........................83

CHAPTER 9...**89**

Developing Adaptability in an AI-Powered Future.......................**89**

    9.1 Building Emotional Intelligence in an AI Environment................ 89

    9.2 Adapting Well to Technological Development............................ 92

    9.3 Investing in Your Career in the AI Age.. 95

CHAPTER 10...**99**

Using AI to Your Advantage for Wealth.. **99**

10.1 Using AI to Advance Your Long-Term Objectives 99

10.2 AI as a Spark for Creativity and Innovation 101

10.3 A Guide to AI-Powered Personal and Business Success 103

ABOUT THE AUTHOR..107

ACKNOWLEDGMENTS

To everyone who helped to create this book, I would like to extend my sincere gratitude.

I want to express my gratitude to my family and friends for their continuous understanding, support, and encouragement throughout this journey. Your confidence in me has consistently inspired me.

I am incredibly appreciative of my mentors and coworkers for sharing their expertise and perspectives, which have improved my comprehension of the complexities of artificial intelligence and its possible effects on our daily lives. Your advice has been really helpful.

We are especially grateful to the AI thought leaders and specialists who so kindly contributed their insights and experiences. The scope and depth of this work have been substantially expanded by your contributions.

I want to express my gratitude to my readers for their interest in and readiness to investigate the potential of artificial intelligence. In both your personal and professional activities, I hope this book encourages you to embrace technology as a potent ally.

Last but not least, I want to thank the innumerable people and institutions who are putting up endless effort to promote the ethical and responsible application of AI. Your dedication to creativity and constructive change is a ray of hope for a better tomorrow.

I appreciate everyone's participation in this adventure.

CHAPTER 1

GETTING TO KNOW AI FEAR

The way we work, live, and interact has changed due to artificial intelligence (AI), which has created both enormous opportunities and a great deal of fear. The phrase "AI anxiety" is frequently used to characterize people's emotional and psychological reactions to the growing influence of AI in many facets of daily life. Understanding AI anxiety's causes, social and psychological repercussions, and prevalence in our culture is essential to comprehending it completely. By exploring these topics in depth, this chapter helps to clarify the nuances of AI adoption and how it affects human experience.

1.1 AI's Ascent and Effects

AI has developed from a sci-fi idea to a game-changing technology that is changing whole sectors. The development of AI can be linked to improvements in big data, algorithm design, and processing power. These days, artificial intelligence (AI) is essential to industries including healthcare, finance, retail, manufacturing, and entertainment. It is transforming everything from predictive analytics to the automation of operations that were previously believed to be solely human.

- **Healthcare:** AI is being applied to robotic surgery, tailored treatments, and illness diagnosis. Although efficiency is increased, there are worries that human judgment may be replaced.

- There are concerns about the loss of traditional financial jobs as a result of the use of AI algorithms in trading, fraud detection, and customer support, which help to streamline processes.

- **Manufacturing:** AI-powered automation contributes to higher productivity and cost effectiveness. But it also raises worries about manual laborers losing their jobs.

- **Customer service:** Chatbots and AI-powered

support systems are replacing human representatives in customer service, speeding up procedures while eliminating the "human touch."

AI has a significant impact since it both stimulates efficiency and creativity and upends established professions and sectors. Uncertainty is increasing when entire career categories are evolving or going extinct. Beyond employment, the emergence of AI affects organizational and governmental decision-making, as it is incorporated into supply chains, security systems, and even policymaking. Even though these advancements are thrilling, they may also be daunting, especially when the technology advances more quickly than laws, educational programs, and workforce development initiatives can keep up.

1.2 The Impact of AI Disruption on the Mind

AI's disruptive potential can have a big psychological impact on people and society. A wide range of emotions are brought about by the development of automation, machine learning, and intelligent systems; some people experience intense worry, while others experience excitement. Numerous psychological responses to the disruptive impact of AI have been noted, such as:

The fear of losing one's job: Many people's main worry is that automation and artificial intelligence will lead to the loss of jobs, especially in industries like manufacturing, customer service, and even white-collar fields like law and medicine. A general feeling of insecurity is brought on by the uncertainty of what positions might be replaced.

- **Loss of influence:** People may feel they have less influence over important areas of their lives as AI grows more independent. Feelings of powerlessness can be exacerbated by the prospect of machines making decisions in the future without human participation.

- **Existential Fear**: Some people may be alarmed by AI's quick development and worry that it may eventually outsmart humans (a theory known as the singularity). A sense that humankind is losing its special position in the world can result from this anxiety.

- **Technological Fatigue**: Burnout may result from the ongoing need to adjust to new tools, platforms, and systems. Workers may feel under pressure to constantly re-skill and upskill as AI develops in order to remain competitive in a labor market that is becoming more automated.

As people try to make sense of their shifting surroundings, these anxieties may lead to elevated levels of stress, anxiety, and even despair. The psychological effects of AI disruption on enterprises can include resistance to change, more staff turnover, and a decline in employee morale, which makes integrating AI into the workplace even more challenging.

1.3 The Surprisingly High Rate of AI Anxiety

AI anxiety is a pervasive issue that impacts people from a wide range of industries, socioeconomic backgrounds, and geographical locations; it is not exclusive to a tiny portion of the population. AI concern is more widespread than most people think for a number of reasons:

- **Lack of Understanding:** Artificial Intelligence is frequently viewed as a "black box" technology that functions in ways that are hard for the general public to comprehend. Because individuals often feel apprehensive about things they do not fully understand, this opacity breeds dread.

- **Rapid Pace of Change:** AI technology is developing at a never-before-seen rate. Today, what was innovative yesterday is no longer relevant. Businesses and individuals find it difficult to keep up with the rapid pace of innovation, which exacerbates feelings of uncertainty and worry.

- **Media Amplification:** Perceptions about AI are greatly influenced by the media. Even if there are a lot of encouraging stories about AI's potential, sensationalist headlines about AI "destroying" mankind, taking over employment, or causing economic disruption are common. This incessant barrage of media might intensify concerns and fears.

- **Cultural and Social Factors:** While technological change is viewed with distrust in certain cultures, it is more easily embraced in others. Social variables also influence how people view and respond to AI, including access to technology and educational attainment. Due to unfamiliarity, AI anxiety may be more noticeable in areas with inadequate technological education.

- **Historical Precedents:** Anxiety related to AI is frequently associated with more general concerns about automation and technological advancement that date back hundreds of years. Similar concerns about robots taking the place of people existed during the industrial revolution, but the possibility that AI could be able to mimic cognitive skills adds a new level of concern.

A fundamental issue with how our society is preparing for and adjusting to technological change is highlighted by the prevalence of AI phobia. In order to allay these concerns, governments, businesses, and educational institutions must act proactively by encouraging AI literacy, encouraging openness in AI research, and establishing safety nets for workers who will be replaced by automation.

Addressing the difficulties brought on by technological advancement requires an understanding of AI fear. While AI presents many potential, it also arouses long-standing anxieties about losing control, losing one's career, and existential issues. AI disruption has profound psychological repercussions that affect how people view their futures in a world that is changing quickly. Furthermore, a lack of information, the speed at which innovation is occurring, media narratives, and cultural attitudes all contribute to the significantly greater prevalence of AI concern than is frequently recognized. In order to ensure that humans do not feel left behind as robots become more intelligent, it is imperative that technological innovation be balanced with initiatives to address the psychological and societal effects of AI.

CHAPTER 2

How Much It Costs to Avoid AI

AI has an unrivaled ability to spur efficiency and innovation across businesses as it develops quickly. However, a lot of people and companies have avoided interacting with AI because of their fear of it and opposition to its inclusion. This avoidance has serious consequences for future success and personal growth in addition to businesses and professions. This chapter examines how avoiding AI results in lost opportunities on both a personal and professional level and explains why ignorance of AI may have long-term negative consequences.

2.1 Lost Chances in Careers and Business

Business executives, entrepreneurs, and professionals may lose out on significant potential if they choose to ignore AI. AI is now a tool for competitive advantage rather than a futuristic idea in today's fast-paced industry. AI has enormous potential to improve decision-making and streamline processes, from automation to data analysis and consumer interaction. In a society that depends more and more on intelligent technology, companies and individuals that are reluctant to embrace AI lag behind.

- **Business Innovation:** Businesses that are afraid of AI are less able to innovate. Businesses can use AI technologies to improve customer experiences through tailored recommendations, automate tedious operations, and identify trends with predictive analytics. Businesses who use AI-driven inventory systems, for instance, can drastically cut waste in the retail industry, while those that do not may face inefficiencies and increased expenses. AI-powered diagnostic tools in the healthcare sector help physicians detect illnesses early on, potentially improving patient outcomes. Businesses who don't use AI lose out on these advancements, which makes it harder for them to stay competitive.

- **Career Development:** Professionals that steer clear

of AI restrict their own professional development. AI-related abilities like machine learning, data analysis, and AI-driven decision-making systems are becoming essential for many high-demand employment areas. Employees risk career stagnation if they stay in traditional roles without learning AI or upskilling. On the other hand, those who use AI technology and keep learning new things are more likely to succeed in their careers, earn more money, and take on leadership responsibilities in their industries.

- o AI abilities are among the most sought-after competencies in the labor market, according to research, and workers who are knowledgeable in AI technology can fetch much greater incomes than their colleagues who are not.

- **Entrepreneurial Ventures:** Business owners that do not incorporate AI into their plans also lose out on expansion prospects. AI can help firms scale quickly by automating marketing campaigns, predicting client demands, and optimizing resources. Without

AI, business owners are forced to make judgments based on sparse data or labor-intensive manual procedures, which hinders their capacity to adjust and expand in cutthroat marketplaces.

In the end, avoiding AI puts you at a competitive disadvantage. The costs are manifested in slowed growth and missed opportunities, whether it's a company that doesn't use AI to streamline operations or a professional who doesn't upgrade their skills to meet future demands.

2.2 The Individual Cost of Avoiding AI

The unwillingness to use AI has an impact on people's personal and professional lives. In a society that is becoming more and more digital, technology is essential to interpersonal relationships, productivity, and general wellbeing. People who avoid AI may suffer from increased stress, strained relationships, and worsened mental health.

- **Increased tension:** Anxiety and tension might result from feeling behind all the time because of a lack of knowledge about AI. This is particularly true for professionals who lack confidence in their ability to use AI in the workplace despite being obligated to do so. Burnout or stress at work might result from the need to "catch up" with AI skills, which can intensify emotions of overwhelm or inadequacy.

- Employees in sectors that are experiencing digital transition may feel as though they are about to become obsolete, which can cause them to become dissatisfied with their jobs, feel useless, or even decide to retire early out of frustration.
- When they observe rivals using AI to make data-driven judgments while they continue to use antiquated techniques, entrepreneurs may also become anxious.

- **Deteriorating connections**: In a world where digital communication and AI-powered gadgets are becoming more and more commonplace, avoiding AI might strain interpersonal connections. AI affects interpersonal relationships and living spaces in a variety of ways, from social media algorithms that influence how we connect with friends and family to smart home appliances that simplify domestic chores. A reluctance to use AI could cause conflict between partners or family members who use new technology and those who don't.

  - Conflicts regarding the place of technology in the home may arise, for instance, if one family member embraces smart home technology to improve household management while another resists.

- **Lost Chances for Individual Development:** AI can improve personal development in the same way that it can benefit professional life. The way people seek self-improvement is being revolutionized by AI-powered applications such as mental health aids, personalized fitness coaches, and virtual learning platforms. People who don't use these tools lose out on chances to expand their abilities, boost their health, or promote personal growth. For instance, people may never take advantage of the possibility to become bilingual if they do not embrace AI-driven language-learning applications.

Avoiding the overpowering nature of artificial intelligence (AI) and technology in general can have a severe impact on mental health. People may feel helpless if they are unaware of AI developments because they may believe they are unable to adapt to changing social norms. As the technological transition continues to impact communication, learning, and information access, the digital gap between those who support AI and those who oppose it can also result in isolation.

2.3 How Failure to Understand AI Will Affect Success in the Future

Ignoring AI's developments can eventually hurt your chances of success in the future. The incapacity to comprehend or adjust to AI will become a more significant obstacle to advancement on both a personal and professional level as it continues to transform sectors and societies.

- **Quickly Shifting Employment Markets:** AI is causing the labor market to change quickly, with positions that were nonexistent ten years ago now in great demand. It may be more difficult for people to move into other positions or even stay relevant in their existing careers if they remain unaware of AI advancements. Adaptability will be essential for future professional success, and AI literacy will play a key role in that. Similar to how digital literacy has grown essential in recent decades, AI abilities will soon be a basic prerequisite in many occupations.

- For instance, positions like as machine learning specialists, data analysts, and AI ethical officers are becoming commonplace across a range of businesses. Those who are unable to comprehend or learn about AI may not be eligible for these chances.

- Entrepreneurs that disregard AI developments run the danger of creating antiquated company strategies. Customers will expect firms to provide AI-driven efficiency, customisation, and responsiveness as AI pervades industries like finance, retail, healthcare, and even education. Businesses that disregard AI risk missing out on funding prospects as investors place a higher priority on projects that are technologically advanced. Businesses are setting the bar by utilizing AI-powered chatbots to improve customer service or predictive analytics to comprehend consumer patterns. Ignoring these trends may cause a company to fall short of customer expectations, which would lower its market share and ultimately lead to failure.

- **Technological Divide:** As society depends more on AI for everything from financial management to medical diagnosis, a gap between people who comprehend AI and those who do not will form. This gap will show up in socioeconomic terms, as people who are more knowledgeable about AI will be able to make better judgments, find better employment prospects, and use AI to enhance both their personal and professional life. Ignoring AI could cause one to lag behind in the digital divide, making it more difficult to access resources and services that will increasingly be powered by AI, as well as employment prospects.

- **Long-term isolation on both a personal and**

professional level: Avoiding AI is about disregarding the way that the world is taking, not just about dismissing a new technology. Future developments, such as tailored medicine and self-driving automobiles, will be built on artificial intelligence. As the divide between people who are comfortable with AI and those who are not grows, refusing to interact with AI could result in long-term isolation. In the workplace, this can entail losing out on prospects for advancement or employment. In one's personal life, it can entail being unable to participate in increasingly AI-driven discussions or activities.

Avoiding AI comes at a significant cost in terms of lost professional and corporate prospects as well as diminished personal wellbeing. Avoiding AI puts up obstacles to creativity, development, and adaptation in a world where technology is changing things quickly. Businesses and individuals lose out on developments that could help them succeed more if they choose not to use AI. Furthermore, as technological competence becomes a standard expectation in both the personal and professional spheres, ignorance of

AI will impede future achievement. Therefore, adopting AI is crucial for navigating and prospering in the future; it is not just a choice.

CHAPTER 3

Converting Fear into Inquisitiveness

It is normal for individuals to feel anxious or afraid when AI technologies develop quickly and start to influence our future more and more. This anxiety frequently results from a lack of knowledge or the belief that AI poses a threat to human autonomy, privacy, or job security. However, people and companies may embrace the amazing possibilities AI presents by turning this fear into interest. Reframing the AI narrative, developing a growth mindset in the AI era, and analyzing actual success stories of people who have used AI to advance their careers and personal lives will all be covered in this chapter.

3.1 Recasting the Story of AI

Recasting the narrative around AI is one of the best strategies to get past people's fear of it. We can start to perceive AI as a potent instrument that improves human potential and fosters creativity rather than as a danger.

- **AI as an Enhancement Tool**: Instead of replacing human skills, AI should be viewed as a supplement. The idea that computers would replace people in a variety of industries is a major source of anxiety regarding AI. Automation may replace routine and repetitive activities, but it can also free up human labor for more strategic, creative, and emotionally intelligent work. AI, for instance, can assist physicians in the healthcare industry by evaluating vast volumes of patient data, enabling them to make better, faster judgments. Instead than taking the place of the doctor, this strengthens their capacity to give care. Similar to this, AI-powered solutions in the creative sectors can help designers and artists by automating technical tasks or coming up with ideas, freeing them up to concentrate on their creative work.

- **AI as an Innovation Catalyst**: AI has the ability to spur innovation across industries and improve human capabilities. Businesses that use AI may solve complicated problems more quickly and accurately, develop more individualized consumer experiences, and open up new business models. For example, AI algorithms in the financial services industry can forecast market trends and direct investment plans, making companies more flexible and sensitive to shifts in the marketplace.

- **Changing from Danger to Possibility**: Realizing that AI, like any other technology, is a tool that is transformed by its use is the first step in changing the perception of AI from one of threat to opportunity. AI has the potential to develop new sectors and job types that we may not completely understand, just like the internet or electricity transformed industries without displacing human labor. By changing our perspective from "what AI might take away" to "what AI can help us achieve," we can take a curious rather than fearful approach to the future.

In the end, realizing that AI is a tool with boundless potential is essential to rewriting the story of AI. It is neither intrinsically good nor harmful, but how we choose to respond to it will determine its effects. We can approach AI with interest, aiming to comprehend and investigate its potential, if we acknowledge that it has the ability to augment human capabilities rather than replace them.

3.2 How to Develop a Growth Mentality in the Age of AI

The idea that abilities and intelligence may be enhanced with diligence, education, and persistence is known as a growth mindset. To thrive in the AI era, where the rate of technological advancement can seem overwhelming, one must have a growth mentality. You'll be more prepared to stay up to date with developments in artificial intelligence and other cutting-edge technology if you embrace the notion that you can adapt and learn.

- **Adopt a Lifelong Learning Attitude:** The idea of lifelong learning is one of the pillars of a growth mindset. This includes aggressively looking for opportunities to learn about AI technology, even if they appear scary at first. This may be reading about

AI applications in your profession, attending workshops, or enrolling in online courses. You will be more equipped to adjust to new technologies as they become available if you adopt an attitude of constant learning.

- **Start with fundamental knowledge:** Although artificial intelligence (AI) can be complicated, a strong foundation can be established by comprehending the fundamentals, such as machine learning, neural networks, and data science.
  - Learn by doing: You may interact directly with AI by experimenting with tools like chatbots or data analysis software, which demystifies the technology and boosts your confidence.

- The development mentality promotes curiosity over perfection, as opposed to a fear of failing. It is hard to attain perfection in the AI era due to the rapid pace of technical breakthroughs. Adopt a curious mindset that welcomes exploration and iteration rather than worrying that you won't be able to master

AI. An entrepreneur might, for instance, experiment with various AI-driven marketing techniques, improving their strategy with each trial.

- **Failure as Feedback:** A growth mindset promotes viewing errors as chances to learn and get better rather than as setbacks. Although there may be a high learning curve with AI, every error presents an opportunity to gain a deeper understanding of the technology and modify your strategy.

- **Remain Adaptable:** In an AI-driven world, the capacity to change course and adapt is more crucial than ever. Having a growth mentality keeps you adaptable and receptive to change. Industries will experience major changes as AI develops further, and those who can adjust to these changes will prosper. Professionals in more automated professions, for example, might need to transition to more creative or strategic work. You may stay ahead of the curve by adjusting to these changes and viewing them as chances for development rather than dangers.

- **Career path flexibility:** As AI takes on increasingly repetitive activities, the nature of jobs will alter. Whether it's upgrading their skills in AI-related fields or moving into new positions where human creativity and empathy are still crucial, people with a growth mindset can change the focus of their careers.

In the AI era, developing a growth mindset frequently entails working with people. This is because AI does not exist in a vacuum. Collaboration broadens your expertise and offers support in navigating AI adoption, whether it be through corporate collaborations, networking with AI professionals, or joining communities focused on AI. You can learn more quickly and get insightful knowledge by interacting with mentors and peers who are also studying AI.

Developing a growth mindset entails accepting lifelong learning, encouraging curiosity, remaining flexible, and working with others. You put yourself in a position to not just survive but also prosper in the AI era by embracing this way of thinking.

3.3 AI Success Story Case Studies

Success stories from the real world show how people and companies have turned their early apprehension about AI into a chance for development and creativity. These illustrations show that AI can be used by businesses of all sizes and in a variety of sectors, making it more than just a tool for big tech firms.

Case Study 1: The AI Transformation of a Retail Chain
- The transformation of a retail chain that initially regarded AI with mistrust is one noteworthy example. The organization was concerned that implementing chatbots for customer care and AI-powered inventory systems would upset their established business model and drive away staff members. However, the business was able to significantly enhance its operations by changing its perspective on AI and viewing it as an enabler rather than a disruptor.
- Predictive analytics powered by AI helped the

business improve product availability and minimize waste by streamlining inventory management.
- AI-powered chatbots improved customer service by providing round-the-clock assistance and responding to consumer inquiries more quickly than human workers.
- The business stated that staff were able to redirect their attention to more fulfilling, customer-facing positions, and that operational efficiency increased by 20% in the first year.

Case Study 2: Innovation in Healthcare and AI
- AI is significantly improving patient care and diagnostic accuracy in the healthcare industry. One hospital used AI-driven diagnostic tools to help clinicians analyze medical imaging since they were initially worried that AI might depersonalize medical care.
- The hospital discovered that AI technologies could identify scan irregularities more quickly and accurately than human radiologists alone, freeing up physicians to concentrate more on patient care and treatment planning. This combination of AI

technology and human knowledge decreased diagnostic errors and enhanced patient outcomes, showing that when AI is carefully incorporated into healthcare, it can strengthen rather than weaken the human component.

Case Study 3: The AI Journey of a Freelancer

- As AI-powered design tools proliferated, a freelance graphic designer first worried that AI would render her skill set outdated. She learned how to employ AI-driven design tools to optimize her productivity, nevertheless, rather than rejecting AI.
- She was able to free up time for more strategic and creative work by using AI to automate repetitive processes like resizing photos, creating design templates, and experimenting with color palettes.
- By using AI to forecast and produce designs that meet future market expectations, this change not only enabled her to take on more customers but also helped her keep ahead of trends in the design business.
- She is now a prominent proponent of AI in the creative sector, educating people on how to integrate

their expertise with AI technology to boost productivity and creativity.

These success stories demonstrate how AI presents enormous potential for innovation and expansion when viewed with curiosity and a growth mentality. AI can be a driver of success in a variety of sectors, including retail, healthcare, and the creative industries, rather than a source of fear or disruption.

It's normal to be afraid of AI, but with the correct attitude, this fear may be turned into opportunity and interest. People and companies can benefit from AI by redefining the AI narrative, developing a growth mindset, and studying successful cases. When we approach artificial intelligence (AI) with curiosity, we can uncover its full potential as a tool for improving human skills. AI is a strong friend on the path to success in the future, not a threat, for those who accept it with flexibility and openness.

CHAPTER 4

USING AI AS A TOOL FOR PERSONAL DEVELOPMENT

Artificial intelligence (AI) is changing not only organizations and industries in the ever changing digital landscape, but also how we approach personal development. AI has the potential to be a tremendous instrument for self-improvement, providing people with access to cutting-edge knowledge, tailored advice, and resources that promote well-being, productivity, and health. AI-driven efficiency is useful, but it's important to keep a healthy balance with technology so that it enhances rather than takes over your life. This chapter will cover ways to strike a healthy balance between AI-driven efficiency and human fulfillment, as well as how AI can be used as a tool for personal growth, health, and well-being.

4.1 AI and Personal Development

A variety of applications provided by AI technologies can

help people in their quest for personal development. AI-powered solutions can offer individualized, data-driven insights that support growth and development, regardless of your goals whether they are to improve your productivity, pick up new skills, or streamline your daily schedule.

The way we learn and develop new talents has been completely transformed by artificial intelligence. AI-powered educational systems can provide personalized learning experiences by using sophisticated algorithms that adjust to different learning preferences. AI is used by platforms like Duolingo, Coursera, and Khan Academy to evaluate a learner's strengths and shortcomings and provide recommendations and personalized content to speed up skill development.

AI can evaluate performance in real time and modify the level of difficulty of assignments or exercises according to a person's development, which makes it easier for them to gain mastery.

Personalized learning routes optimize the learning process and lessen frustration by ensuring that users spend more time concentrating on areas where they need to improve.

AI-powered language learning applications, for example, can make learning a new language more effective and interesting by assisting users with pronunciation practice, context-based vocabulary suggestions, and accurate progress tracking.

Increased Productivity with AI Tools: With a range of task management tools, intelligent reminders, and AI-powered scheduling applications, AI can assist people in streamlining their daily schedules and increasing productivity. AI can recommend methods to automate repetitive processes and prioritize tasks by examining workload and behavior patterns, freeing up time for more important pursuits.

- AI-powered personal assistants, like Google Assistant and Apple's Siri, may automate daily chores by arranging appointments, sending reminders, and even writing emails in response to commands. This enables people to avoid becoming mired down in mundane chores and instead concentrate on higher-level strategic work.
- AI is used by productivity apps such as Notion or Todoist to track progress over time, recommend

priorities, and organize workflows. These tools can assist users in pinpointing areas where they might increase their efficiency or sharpen their attention by analyzing their particular work patterns.

- Additionally, financial management functions like investing and budgeting can be automated with AI. Artificial intelligence (AI) algorithms are used by programs like Mint and Personal Capital to classify spending, analyze spending patterns, and offer tailored financial advice that assists users in achieving their financial objectives.

AI-Driven Creativity: AI can be a useful tool for inspiration and idea generation for people looking to improve their creativity. Tools that can help with the design process, create fresh ideas, or offer creative solutions include Canva's AI design assistant and OpenAI's GPT.

- For instance, writers can overcome creative blockages and increase productivity by using AI tools to produce outlines, brainstorm ideas, and even draft sections of content.
- AI enables designers to test out various layouts, color palettes, and visual components, enabling more

imaginative exploration in less time.

People can learn more quickly, be more creative, and be more productive by using AI for self-improvement. This will help them accomplish their goals more quickly, both personally and professionally.

4.2 AI in Wellness and Health

AI is also changing how we think about health and wellbeing by providing data-driven, individualized insights that can enhance both physical and emotional well-being. These technologies, which range from chatbots for mental health to fitness apps driven by AI, are improving the efficiency, accessibility, and personalization of health management.

Personalized Fitness and Nutrition: Fitbit, MyFitnessPal, Strava, and other AI-powered fitness apps are transforming the way people think about fitness by giving them real-time data on their heart rates, activity levels, and calorie intake. These apps include progress tracking, individualized exercise regimens, and dietary guidance based on data from wearable technology.

- Fitness coaches with AI capabilities are able to examine a person's activity patterns, provide customized training plans, and even modify advice in response to performance or injury.
- In terms of nutrition, AI may monitor daily food consumption and recommend meal plans that support dietary objectives, such as maintaining a balanced diet, gaining muscle, or losing weight. With regular monitoring and tailored feedback, these solutions not only save time but also improve the likelihood of reaching health goals.

AI in Mental Health assistance: Natural language processing is used by AI-powered mental health platforms like Woebot and Wysa to provide chatbots that provide mental health assistance and cognitive behavioral therapy (CBT) approaches. By providing a secure environment for individuals to communicate their emotions and get immediate response, these tools make mental health care easily accessible and reasonably priced.

- These artificial intelligence (AI) tools can assist users in monitoring their emotions, recognizing anxious or depressive symptoms, and providing tailored coping mechanisms.

- Because users can get help discreetly and at their own pace without the strain of face-to-face conversations, AI-powered mental health apps are also helpful in lowering stigma.
- AI can make better recommendations over time by using interaction data, eventually providing more sophisticated and successful mental health treatments.

AI in Mindfulness and Stress Management: AI-powered mindfulness applications like Calm and Headspace are assisting people in managing stress with customized meditation regimens and relaxation techniques. Stress is a common problem in modern living. These applications can determine a user's stress and mood and provide specific relaxation treatments like breathing exercises, guided meditation, or visualizations.

- In order to better customize mindfulness exercises to each user's needs and make sure they receive the best interventions for their unique stress levels, AI can also use data from wearables, such as heart rate

or sleep habits.
- By encouraging long-term mental resilience and emotional well-being, these tools assist users in developing enduring mindfulness practices.

By incorporating AI into health and well-being, people can take charge of their mental and physical health and use data-driven insights and tailored suggestions to lead more balanced, healthier lives.

4.3 Harmonizing AI and Individual Satisfaction

Even though AI has the potential to greatly improve productivity, well-being, and efficiency, it's important to strike a good balance between utilizing AI-driven solutions and keeping personal pleasure. The intention is to make sure that technology facilitates personal development without diminishing the significance of interpersonal relationships, creativity, and self-awareness.

AI as a Facilitator, Not a Substitute: Though AI can improve many facets of life, it shouldn't take the place of fundamental human experiences like forming bonds with others, expressing oneself creatively, or following one's passions. The efficiency that AI provides should allow people to devote more time to fulfilling and joyful pursuits, like hobbies, new experiences, and time spent with loved ones.

- AI-powered tools, for example, can assist in managing a hectic work schedule, but it's crucial to establish boundaries that provide relaxation and introspection. An excessive dependence on artificial intelligence (AI) for decision-making can occasionally result in a loss of emotional intelligence and personal intuition, both of which are essential for a happy existence.

How to Use Technology While Maintaining a Mindful Lifestyle: Keeping a healthy balance between AI-driven productivity and individual well being requires mindfulness. It's important to be aware of when and how to use AI. Maintaining mental clarity and emotional equilibrium can be achieved by scheduling daily time to unplug from electronics, exercise, or just think.

- You can stop technology from taking over your life by setting limits on screen time and being deliberate about how AI is incorporated into everyday activities.

- Reconnecting with oneself and one's surroundings through digital detoxes taking a vacation from artificial intelligence and digital tools can promote higher personal fulfillment and lessen reliance on technology.

Putting Human Connection First: Although AI can automate a lot of jobs, nothing can take the place of human connection. A fulfilling existence requires developing empathy, cultivating meaningful relationships, and honing emotional intelligence. While AI tools can help with communication and teamwork, real human interaction is necessary for personal development.

- For instance, it can be effective to use AI to handle communication chores, but in order to preserve deep emotional bonds and foster trust, in both personal and professional relationships, it is crucial to prioritize in-person encounters. Achieving objectives is simply one aspect of personal fulfillment; another is cultivating connections that offer encouragement, happiness, and meaning. Maintaining a healthy balance between technology use and real human interaction guarantees that AI complements these essential facets of life rather than takes their place.

It's critical to maintain a healthy balance even if AI can greatly improve personal growth by maximizing productivity, promoting health, and enhancing well-being. AI should be viewed as a tool that helps people realize their potential, but it should never take precedence over the value of interpersonal relationships, creativity, and personal fulfillment. People can profit from AI while maintaining a meaningful, balanced, and purposeful life by employing it purposefully and thoughtfully.

CHAPTER 5

USING AI TO GROW YOUR COMPANY

From a futuristic idea, artificial intelligence (AI) has developed into a vital tool for companies looking to stay competitive in a market that is changing quickly. Businesses may increase productivity, enhance customer satisfaction, and make better strategic decisions by utilizing AI. Businesses have a clear edge when they can automate repetitive tasks, provide individualized consumer interactions, and analyze enormous volumes of data in real-time. This chapter will examine how artificial intelligence (AI) can be used to improve decision-making, streamline processes, and raise customer satisfaction levels in order to grow your organization.

5.1 Using AI to Make Strategic Decisions

By analyzing massive datasets, finding patterns, and forecasting future events with previously unheard-of accuracy, artificial intelligence (AI) enables business executives to make more informed decisions. With the use of this skill, decision-making becomes proactive and forward-looking rather than frequently reactive and dependent on incomplete information.

The ability of AI algorithms to process and analyze vast amounts of both structured and unstructured data allows them to provide insights that are not possible to obtain through conventional methods. As a result, leaders are able to make better judgments based on current information rather than just gut feeling or past trends.

Analytics platforms with AI capabilities can look at internal performance indicators, market trends, and consumer behavior to provide useful information that informs business strategy.

Businesses can make proactive decisions that reduce risk and grab opportunities before rivals do by using predictive analytics to foresee market shifts, client demands, and possible hazards.

Scenario Planning and Forecasting: AI systems support scenario analysis as well, enabling companies to model various approaches and predict their possible results. This is particularly helpful in sectors like retail, finance, and healthcare where market conditions can shift quickly.

- An AI system, for example, can simulate several new product launch scenarios while taking into account different market conditions, customer trends, and rivalry. Business executives can increase the likelihood of success by selecting the best course of action based on these insights.
- AI-powered financial modeling tools can offer comprehensive cash flow, cost, and revenue forecasts, assisting businesses in making data-supported strategic acquisitions or sales.

Enhanced Risk Management: AI helps companies recognize and control hazards more effectively. AI may identify trends that could indicate possible dangers or vulnerabilities, whether in the fields of cybersecurity in IT, fraud detection in finance, or predictive maintenance in manufacturing.

- Real-time transactional data analysis using AI can spot suspect patterns or fraudulent activity, enabling prompt action to reduce losses.

- AI in supply chain management can foresee interruptions brought on by things like natural disasters, logistical delays, or geopolitical unrest, allowing companies to make preemptive strategy adjustments.

Businesses may adopt a more dynamic, data-driven mindset and move past conventional, retrospective approaches to strategic decision-making by integrating AI. Better decision-making, more agility, and a stronger competitive position result from this.

5.2 Using AI to Simplify Operations

For companies looking to expand, save expenses, and concentrate on innovation, operational efficiency is crucial. By automating repetitive, everyday work, artificial intelligence (AI) frees up resources to concentrate on high-level strategic endeavors. AI-driven process optimization can also speed up operations, lower errors, and enhance quality.

Automation of Routine Tasks: AI is excellent at

managing time-consuming, repetitive tasks that are essential to day-to-day operations but don't always call for human creativity or judgment. Data input, billing, payroll, customer service inquiries, and other tasks are included in this.

- One type of AI that automates rule-based operations is called robotic process automation, or RPA. AI, for instance, may handle simple client inquiries, conduct transactions, and automatically generate reports, greatly lowering the administrative load on staff members.
- Robots driven by AI can perform assembly line duties in sectors like manufacturing, guaranteeing accuracy and speed. This improves operational uptime and output rates while also lowering human error.

Supply Chain and Inventory Management: By evaluating data to forecast demand, control inventory levels, and guarantee effective logistics, artificial intelligence (AI) can improve supply chain management.

- To predict inventory needs, machine learning algorithms might examine past sales data, customer

habits, and outside variables (such as economic conditions or seasonal demand). This minimizes stockouts and overstock scenarios by guaranteeing that companies have the appropriate supplies on hand when they're needed.
- By evaluating real-time data from traffic, weather, and other factors, AI-driven logistics solutions can reduce transportation costs, forecast shipping delays, and improve delivery routes.

Workforce Optimization: By forecasting staffing requirements, enhancing scheduling, and evaluating employee performance, AI may be utilized to optimize workforce management.
- The proper amount of workers are available to meet demand while preventing overstaffing at slower times thanks to AI-driven scheduling technologies that can anticipate busy times and assign workers appropriately.
- AI can detect skill shortages, suggest training courses, and even determine which workers are most likely to experience burnout or disengagement by evaluating employee performance data. This enables

managers to take preventative measures.

Businesses can streamline operations, cut expenses, and reallocate resources to innovation and expansion by automating repetitive tasks and streamlining procedures. Businesses may function more effectively thanks to AI, which lays the groundwork for growth and a competitive edge.

5.3 Using AI to Improve Customer Experience

Consumers of today need smooth, responsive, and customized brand encounters. By offering personalized recommendations, quicker service, and intelligent support systems, artificial intelligence (AI) is a potent tool for enhancing the customer experience. Businesses may improve customer happiness, foster loyalty, and forge closer bonds with their clients by utilizing AI.

Personalization at Scale: By evaluating information about consumers' interests, actions, and past purchases, AI enables companies to provide them with incredibly tailored experiences.

- Artificial intelligence (AI)-powered recommendation engines, like those employed by Netflix and Amazon, examine a user's past purchases and browsing activity to make recommendations for goods or entertainment that fit their preferences. By providing tailored recommendations, this improves the overall client experience and raises the possibility of conversions.
- By choosing products based on a customer's previous purchases, search history, and even demographic information, artificial intelligence (AI) in e-commerce can produce individualized shopping experiences. This degree of customization boosts consumer satisfaction and encourages recurring business.

Enhancing Reaction Times using AI Chatbots: Chatbots and virtual assistants driven by AI are revolutionizing how companies provide customer service. By instantly responding to consumer questions, these systems can drastically cut down on wait times and enhance the general customer experience.

- AI chatbots can answer a variety of questions,

ranging from basic product details to more intricate troubleshooting problems. This lessens the workload for human customer support representatives, freeing them up to concentrate on higher-level duties while guaranteeing that clients receive prompt responses.

- Artificial intelligence (AI) chatbots can continuously enhance their comprehension and response to consumer inquiries by utilizing machine learning and natural language processing (NLP). Additionally, they can be integrated with CRM systems to offer tailored responses according to the client's past interactions with the business.

AI in Predictive Customer Service: AI is able to predict the demands of customers before they materialize, providing proactive support that resolves problems before they become complaints.

- Patterns in consumer behavior that indicate discontent or possible attrition can be found using predictive analytics. AI can, for instance, initiate an automated outreach to follow up with a customer and offer support or incentives to re-engage them if their use of a product or service declines.

- Businesses may proactively meet customer demands and lower the chance of discontent by using AI to forecast when products or services might need maintenance or replacement.

Improved Customer Feedback and Sentiment Analysis: AI can assist companies in better analyzing customer feedback by spotting sentiments and trends that manual analysis might miss.

- Customer reviews, social media posts, and support complaints can all be combed through by AI-driven sentiment analysis tools to find recurring themes or problems that require attention. This enables companies to address customer issues and take remedial action when needed more rapidly.
- Businesses may enhance their goods, services, and general customer experience by knowing the general tone of consumer interactions.

Businesses may not only meet but also surpass customer expectations by utilizing AI to improve the customer experience. Businesses can now provide intelligent, responsive, and personalized services at scale thanks to AI, which boosts client loyalty and happiness and, eventually, corporate performance.

AI has the potential to revolutionize enterprises in a variety of sectors. Businesses can obtain a substantial competitive advantage by utilizing AI to improve consumer experiences, streamline operations, and make strategic decisions. AI is not simply a tool for efficiency in today's fast-paced industry; it is an essential resource for success, growth, and innovation. enterprises who invest in AI's capabilities will be well-positioned to dominate their respective industries as it continues to be adopted by enterprises, creating both immediate and long-term value.

CHAPTER 6

BREAKING DOWN BUSINESS BARRIERS TO AI ADOPTION

It is commonly known that incorporating artificial intelligence (AI) into company operations has several advantages, including better decision-making, increased operational effectiveness, and improved consumer experiences. Nevertheless, many firms find it difficult to completely embrace AI in spite of these benefits. Adoption of AI is hampered by a number of factors, including cultural, financial, and technological ones. Companies must identify these obstacles, develop a workforce prepared for AI, and foster strong leadership that steers the change in order to successfully integrate AI. The common obstacles to AI adoption will be discussed in this chapter, along with strategies for assembling a team ready for AI integration and the crucial role that leadership plays in overcoming these obstacles.

6.1 Recognizing Typical Obstacles to AI Adoption

A company must first determine the most common obstacles that impede or delay adoption of AI before it can overcome these challenges. These challenges frequently fall under a number of categories, such as technological, cultural, and financial ones. If left unchecked, these issues might prevent a business from fully utilizing AI.

Costs and Return on Investment Issues: The initial expense of AI technology is one of the main obstacles that companies must overcome. Significant investment is frequently needed for AI systems, infrastructure, and the skilled personnel required to create and operate these systems.

- Many businesses, especially small and medium-sized businesses (SMEs), may be reluctant to engage in AI because they believe the ROI is uncertain or could take years to show results.
- Adoption of AI also necessitates a sustained investment in hardware, software, and cloud storage, which raises continuing operating expenses. Companies have to weigh these expenses against

possible long-term savings and efficiencies.

Lack of Technical Expertise: AI is a complicated topic that calls for specific expertise in data engineering, data science, and machine learning. Finding and keeping the proper people is a big challenge for many companies.

- Smaller businesses or those not in tech-related fields might not have the funds to upskill their current employees or acquire AI specialists. This problem is made worse by the lack of qualified AI workers available on the market, which increases competition for talent and raises hiring expenses.

Data Challenges: In order to train algorithms and produce precise insights, artificial intelligence depends on enormous volumes of high-quality data. Data silos, in which information is kept in several systems and is challenging to access and integrate for AI usage, are among the data-related problems that many firms face.

- Inaccurate or incomplete datasets are examples of poor data quality, which can result in AI predictions and outputs that are not trustworthy.
- Data security and privacy issues, especially in light

of laws like the GDPR that mandate businesses handle and safeguard customer data with care.

opposition to Change: One of the hardest obstacles to overcome is cultural opposition. Workers may be reluctant to embrace new technologies because they don't understand or feel comfortable using them, or they may worry that AI will replace their work.

- Companies may not embrace AI as rapidly as they could due to organizational inertia, particularly in sectors that have historically relied on manual procedures or that are sluggish to adapt new technologies.
- Staff or leadership may become skeptical and push back if they believe AI will make judgments on its own without human supervision.

The first step to getting past these obstacles is realizing what they are. Businesses may eliminate barriers and create the conditions for a seamless AI adoption process by methodically tackling each difficulty.

6.2 Creating a Team Prepared for AI

A team with the necessary abilities and mentality to effectively utilize AI's potential is necessary for the successful integration of AI into a business; technology alone is not enough. Upskilling, encouraging an innovative culture, and making sure staff members are at ease with the shift to AI-enhanced operations are all necessary to develop a workforce that is prepared for AI.

Skill Development and Training: Investing in training and development is one of the most important ways to get a team ready for integrating AI.

- **Upskilling:** Workers must learn how AI will affect their jobs and how to collaborate with new technologies. Employees who will work directly with AI systems must have training in data literacy, AI technologies, and fundamental machine learning concepts.
- **Cross-functional collaboration:** Data science, IT, operations, and marketing are just a few of the departments that must work together to apply AI. A more unified approach to AI adoption can be

achieved by cross-training staff members to comprehend how AI fits into different business domains.

- **External partnerships:** Businesses can work with universities, AI research centers, or consultants to develop expertise within the firm when internal resources are scarce.

Cultivating a Culture of Innovation: Technical training alone is not enough to create a team that is prepared for AI. It also entails cultivating an environment that values trial and error, education, and flexibility.

- Companies ought to establish a secure setting where staff members can test AI solutions without worrying about failing. Before a full-scale rollout, AI can be tested in particular business domains through pilot projects and trial implementations.
- Addressing employees' worries about AI requires open communication. Leaders should explain in detail how AI will enhance and supplement responsibilities rather than replace them, emphasizing chances for workers to be more productive and innovative.

- Instead of opposing AI, employees will embrace it if they are encouraged to adopt a growth mentality and are receptive to lifelong learning. This attitude can be further strengthened by praising and rewarding staff members who adopt new technologies and participate in AI initiatives.

Human-AI Collaboration: An AI-ready team recognizes that AI is a tool to enhance human capabilities rather than a substitute for human labor.

- Encourage staff members to see AI as a way to improve their positions. AI, for example, can automate repetitive operations so that workers can concentrate on more creative or strategic elements of their jobs.
- AI adoption will be smooth and successful if staff members are trained to understand AI-driven insights and make defensible decisions based on them.

Businesses may maximize the benefits of AI and speed up its integration by assembling a staff that is both technically proficient and receptive to the technology.

6.3 Leadership's Significance in AI Integration

Overcoming the obstacles of AI adoption requires strong leadership. In addition to being knowledgeable on AI's technological features, business executives need to have the foresight and clout to lead their companies through the challenges of digital transformation. Driving change, overcoming opposition, and guaranteeing the successful integration of AI all depend heavily on leadership.

AI as a Strategic Priority: Rather than being a stand-alone project, leaders need to see AI as a fundamental part of the organization's long-term strategy.

- AI activities should be in line with the organization's objectives, whether those be increasing customer pleasure, cutting expenses, or spurring innovation, and should be incorporated into the entire business plan.
- Leaders must determine the most valuable applications of AI and set investment priorities appropriately. Customer service, supply chain management, and sales forecasting are a few

examples of this.

Championing AI Adoption: To set the example for the rest of the company, leadership must aggressively promote AI adoption.
- As role models, company executives should show that they are dedicated to learning about AI and promoting its advantages throughout the organization.
- Leadership that communicates openly can allay worries or mistrust around AI. This entails being transparent about how AI may affect employment, processes, and corporate culture while emphasizing how technology will ultimately help the organization and its workers.

Overcoming Opposition and Managing Change: Resistance to change is one of the main barriers to the adoption of AI, and it is the responsibility of leadership to successfully handle this.
- Leaders must create an atmosphere where workers are encouraged to embrace AI rather than be afraid of it. To address issues and showcase achievements

from other divisions or businesses, this may entail holding town halls, workshops, or Q&A sessions.

- Employees may better grasp the phases of AI integration and their role at each level with the use of change management techniques like developing an AI adoption roadmap. This lessens employees' fear of the unknown and helps them understand how AI will affect their day-to-day work.

Ethical Considerations and Responsible AI Use: To guarantee that AI is applied in a responsible and ethical way, strong leadership is also necessary.

- In order to ensure that AI is used ethically and in accordance with the company's values and legal requirements, leaders should establish explicit guidelines. This involves tackling issues with bias in AI algorithms, data privacy, and the possible effects of automation on society.

- It's also crucial to guarantee transparency in AI decision-making. To ensure that workers, clients, and stakeholders have faith in the company's AI projects, leaders should encourage openness in the usage of AI systems and the decision-making process.

The key to the successful implementation of AI is leadership. Businesses may overcome opposition, incorporate AI into their strategic vision, and make sure that AI benefits the company rather than detracts from it if they have visionary and dedicated leaders at the helm.

A comprehensive strategy that tackles both technological and cultural issues is needed to remove obstacles to AI adoption. The first step for businesses is to identify typical obstacles, such as aversion to change, talent gaps, and financial constraints. Developing a workforce that is knowledgeable, flexible, and receptive to new ideas is vital, and leadership is vital in promoting acceptance, controlling change, and guaranteeing the moral use of AI. Businesses may fully utilize AI if the proper plans are in place, turning challenges into chances for expansion, productivity, and a competitive edge.

CHAPTER 7

ETHICAL AI: ALIGNING TECHNOLOGY WITH VALUES E

There are now more chances for productivity, creativity, and expansion thanks to the quick development and application of AI technology in business. To guarantee that AI systems are in line with social values and corporate ethics, however, these advantages come with serious ethical issues that need to be resolved. In addition to being required by law, ethical AI is essential for fostering trust among stakeholders, employees, and customers. This chapter examines the moral dilemmas raised by AI, responsible AI implementation strategies for companies, and the importance of responsibility in AI-driven decision-making.

7.1 Comprehending AI's Ethical Difficulties

Businesses are spending more and more on AI, thus it's critical to comprehend the moral dilemmas raised by this potent technology. To guarantee justice, accountability, and trust, ethical considerations must be at the forefront of AI development and use. The following are a few of the most urgent ethical issues:

Bias in AI Algorithms: The possibility of bias in algorithms is one of the biggest ethical issues facing AI. Because AI systems can only be as objective as the data they are educated on, biased data will be reinforced by the AI.
- Discriminatory outcomes in fields such as recruiting, financing, law enforcement, and healthcare might result from algorithmic bias.
- An AI hiring tool educated on past hiring data, for instance, can unjustly disadvantage some groups by reproducing historical racial or gender biases.
- Businesses must make sure that their data sets are representative, diversified, and subject to frequent fairness audits in order to combat bias.

Privacy Concerns: AI systems use enormous volumes of data, frequently containing private and sensitive information. This calls into question the methods utilized to gather, store, and use data.

- Regulations such as the California Consumer Privacy Act (CCPA) and the General Data Protection Regulation (GDPR) have made the ethical concern of data privacy even more pressing.
- By putting in place robust data protection mechanisms, restricting data gathering to what is required, and being open and honest about data usage, businesses can make sure AI systems respect people's privacy.
- The difficulty lies in striking a balance between protecting privacy and adhering to legal requirements while using data to enhance AI systems.

The openness of AI decision-making The lack of transparency in the decision-making process of AI systems is known as the "black box" problem of AI. Trust is damaged when AI systems function without providing explicit explanations, making it challenging to comprehend why particular results happen.

- For example, a customer can feel unfairly treated if an AI system rejects their loan application without

giving them a clear explanation.
- In order to make AI decision-making more transparent and intelligible to humans, businesses should prioritize explainability by implementing "explainable AI" models.

The application of AI in decision-making processes that have an impact on people's lives can have a substantial impact on human autonomy.
- If decisions are made without sufficient human monitoring, automated decision-making in domains like credit scoring, hiring, or even court rulings may compromise individual rights.
- Companies need to make sure AI systems are not only effective but also equitable and considerate of people's rights to contest choices or, if needed, seek human intervention.

Businesses must comprehend these moral dilemmas in order to adhere to legal requirements and preserve their reputation for using AI in a morally and responsibly manner. By addressing these problems early on, long-term hazards can be avoided and a reliable AI environment can be developed.

7.2 Making Responsible Use of AI in Your Company

Any company looking to incorporate AI technologies into its operations must make sure that they are used appropriately. Beyond merely staying out of trouble with the law, responsible AI entails incorporating moral principles into the development and application of AI systems. Businesses should follow these guidelines to use AI responsibly:

Establishing a clear set of ethical guidelines that are in line with your company's values and industry best practices is the first step towards using AI responsibly.
- Create ethical AI guidelines that address issues such as accountability, transparency, privacy, and justice.
- These recommendations ought to be incorporated throughout every stage of the AI development process, from gathering data and training models to deploying the system and conducting continuous monitoring.
- Businesses should think about setting up a AI ethics

committee to examine AI initiatives and make sure they adhere to moral principles.

Implement Fairness and Inclusivity: Companies must put in place procedures that support fairness and inclusivity in AI applications in order to mitigate the danger of bias.
- It is possible to audit AI systems and find possible places where the model can generate discriminatory results by using bias detection tools.
- Retraining models over time guarantees that they continue to learn from more representative data, and regularly testing AI systems with a variety of data sets can help minimize bias.
- Creating inclusive AI teams with a variety of viewpoints will also assist guarantee that AI systems represent a greater range of demands and experiences.

The implementation of transparent AI practices An essential element of using AI responsibly is transparency. Companies must make sure that their AI systems are both efficient and comprehensible.
- Put into practice explainable AI models that offer

concise justifications for the choices they make, especially in high-stakes domains like law enforcement, healthcare, and finance.
- Being open and honest with stakeholders and customers about the company's use of AI and the data being gathered is another aspect of transparency.
- For instance, the company should notify customers and provide them the option to opt out if AI is being used to evaluate user behavior or make product recommendations.

Respect User Rights: When AI is used to make decisions that affect people's lives, it is extremely important that it respects their rights.
- Make sure AI systems give users the choice of human review when making important decisions like hiring, approving credit, or making decisions about the law.
- In order to ensure that AI does not deprive people of their personal agency or the ability to challenge results, businesses should also put in place appeals processes for people who want to challenge

judgments made by AI.

Regular Ethical Audits: To make sure AI systems continue to function morally as they develop and absorb new information, they should be subjected to frequent audits.

- Audits should evaluate how effectively the AI system performs in terms of accountability, openness, and fairness as well as how well it complies with data privacy laws.
- Continuous monitoring aids in spotting any emerging ethical concerns that may surface when the AI system is used in novel settings or is exposed to various kinds of data.

Responsible AI use entails incorporating moral principles into every stage of the creation and application of AI. Businesses can make sure that their AI solutions not only boost productivity and creativity but also help create a just, equitable, and reliable digital future by following these guidelines.

7.3 Accountability's Function in AI-Powered Decision Making

The issue of accountability is becoming more urgent as AI is incorporated into corporate processes more and more. To avoid harm and preserve trust, human oversight and clear lines of accountability are crucial when AI systems are used to make important decisions.

Human Oversight of AI: AI systems should not be used alone for important business decisions, even though they are more efficient than humans in processing vast amounts of data and making choices.

- AI should not be considered a decision-maker, but rather a decision-support tool. For AI-driven judgments to be in line with moral principles and corporate objectives, human monitoring is essential.
- AI algorithms may identify possible fraud in the financial services industry, for instance, but a person should make the final decision because they are better able to understand the AI's results in light of the customer's past actions and history.

Explicit Responsibility for AI Outcomes: Companies need to set up explicit accountability for the results of AI-driven choices, especially in fields where the ramifications might be severe, like law enforcement, healthcare, and finance.

- Businesses that remove themselves from the moral ramifications of AI acts may experience moral disengagement as a result of a lack of accountability. Companies should assign particular teams or persons to supervise AI implementations in order to prevent this.
- These teams should have the skills and power to step in when AI systems yield unfavorable or immoral results, guaranteeing that humans continue to bear the primary responsibility for AI choices.

Ethical Accountability Structures: It is imperative to create official frameworks for AI accountability. This could entail setting up AI governance committees or AI ethics boards to supervise the moral use of AI across the company.

- Regular reviews of AI deployments, risk

assessments, and verification that AI systems are functioning in accordance with the organization's ethical standards and values should all be part of these structures.

- Additionally, companies ought to think about establishing whistleblower mechanisms that allow staff members to voice concerns with AI procedures or results without worrying about facing reprisals. This promotes a culture of ongoing development and ethical awareness.

Liability and Legal Considerations: As AI systems grow increasingly integral to corporate processes, liability issues become more complicated. When an AI system makes a mistake or its decisions have negative effects, who bears the blame?

- Companies need to make sure they have a clear legal framework in place to handle liability concerns pertaining to AI. In order to reflect the changing role of AI in decision-making, this may include revising contracts, regulations, and legal agreements.
- Businesses can also defend themselves against legal lawsuits by keeping documentation of AI

decision-making procedures and guaranteeing openness in the decision-making process.

An essential component of using AI ethically is accountability. Businesses can reduce risks and preserve stakeholder, employee, and consumer trust by implementing formal accountability frameworks, ensuring transparency in AI-driven decisions, and maintaining explicit human oversight.

In addition to being a technical difficulty, ethical AI is now a strategic and cultural requirement for companies. Businesses must address the ethical issues of prejudice, privacy, and transparency as AI systems are incorporated more deeply into decision-making processes. They must also make sure that their AI applications are consistent with larger society ideals. Clear ethical standards, equity, inclusion, openness, and respect for user rights are necessary for the responsible use of AI. Additionally,

Accountability is essential to guaranteeing the morality and reliability of AI-driven decisions. Businesses may take the lead in creating AI solutions that not only spur innovation but also adhere to the highest ethical standards by incorporating these principles into their AI plans.

CHAPTER 8

SUCCEEDING WITH AI WITHOUT COMPROMISE ON WELL-BEING

Numerous chances for efficiency, creativity, and productivity have been made possible by the widespread use of AI technology in both business and daily life. But these developments also bring with them the difficulty of using AI in ways that don't jeopardize individual wellbeing. This chapter will examine how to use AI tools for personal time management, preserve the human relationships that are crucial in a technologically advanced environment, and achieve AI-driven success while leading a balanced life. The goal is to use AI to improve both life and business, not at the price of meaningful relationships, work-life balance, or mental health.

8.1 Combining AI with a Well-Being Lifestyle

AI is permeating every aspect of our everyday lives, from

personal devices intended to increase productivity to business automation solutions. Although artificial intelligence (AI) has the potential to revolutionize our way of life and work, there is growing worry that pursuing success through AI may result in stress, burnout, and an unhealthful work-life balance. Thoughtful integration of AI into our daily lives is necessary to balance its advantages with human welfare.

Avoiding AI Overload: Making sure AI technologies increase productivity without adding to stress is one of the main issues. Although AI is capable of processing enormous volumes of data and streamlining processes, its constant availability can also result in information overload and overwork.

- Setting boundaries with technology is crucial. One way to stop work from intruding into personal time is to restrict notifications from AI-powered systems during non-work hours. In a similar vein, blocking aside personal time using AI-driven scheduling tools is a proactive approach to safeguard wellbeing.
- Both individuals and employees should refrain from making decisions only based on AI tools.

Over-reliance on AI can impair critical thinking and problem-solving abilities. Finding a balance between human intuition and AI support is essential.

On the other hand, AI provides a number of wellness applications that can enhance both physical and mental well-being. Apps with AI capabilities, such as sleep trackers, fitness monitors, and calming meditation tools, can help reduce stress and enhance general wellness.

- AI-powered applications such as Calm and Headspace, for example, employ data-driven insights to provide customized meditation sessions that lower stress and improve mental clarity.
- AI-powered fitness monitors can give users immediate feedback on their physical activity, motivating them to maintain an active lifestyle and give self-care first priority all day long.

Workload Reduction through Automation: The ability of AI to automate repetitive tasks is one of its main benefits in both personal and professional situations. AI facilitates the creation of more innovative and significant activities by relieving people of repetitive or time-consuming duties.

- AI-powered automation solutions in the workplace may manage customer inquiries and sort emails, freeing up specialists to work on higher-value duties.
- Daily tasks can be streamlined at home using automation. AI-enabled gadgets, such as smart home assistants, can assist with scheduling, reminding people, and even automating grocery shopping.

The secret to successfully incorporating AI into daily life is to use it as a tool to improve balance rather than to push oneself too far. When AI is used thoughtfully, people can manage their workloads, focus on their career and personal development, and experience less stress.

8.2 AI Time Management Tools for Individuals

Time management is one of the most beneficial ways AI can promote wellbeing. Effective time management might feel difficult due to the abundance of responsibilities and distractions vying for attention in both personal and professional life. Thankfully, AI-powered time management solutions can assist in effectively prioritizing chores and streamlining daily plans.

AI-Powered Task Management Systems: Numerous AI programs are made to assist people in better managing their calendars and responsibilities. AI is used by programs like Trello, Monday.com, and Asana to streamline processes, determine priorities, and recommend the most effective approach to do tasks. These platforms automatically generate schedules that help balance work while making sure that critical tasks are given priority by using artificial intelligence (AI) to analyze tasks and deadlines. By doing this, users may stay focused and lower their chance of becoming overburdened by attempting to perform too many things at once.

- Additionally, AI can monitor development in real time, providing information about potential inefficiencies and enabling users to modify their schedules to maximize output without adding to stress.

Time-Blocking with AI: Time-blocking is a time-management strategy that entails breaking the day up into time slots for particular activities or tasks. This procedure can be automated with the use of AI technologies such as Google Calendar and Clockwise, which can intelligently identify open time slots and schedule work according to deadlines and priorities. These methods guarantee that there is time set apart for breaks, personal pursuits, and family obligations in addition to helping to block off time for concentrated work. Time-blocking enabled by AI increases productivity by promoting concentrated work intervals interspersed with recuperation time, which is critical for mental health.

AI for Distraction and Focus Management: It might be difficult to maintain concentration in the digital world of today. Artificial intelligence (AI) technologies such as RescueTime and Focus@Will are made to assist people in reducing distractions and focusing while at work.

- AI is used by RescueTime to examine how people spend their time on digital devices and reveal which activities take up the most time. In order to help you stay focused during work hours, it can also block distracting websites and apps.
- Comparably, Focus@Will makes use of AI-powered soundtracks that are scientifically proven to improve

focus and reduce distractions, making it simpler to sustain productivity while lowering mental exhaustion.

AI Scheduling Assistants with Personalization: AI is used by programs like x.ai and Clara to act as virtual scheduling assistants. For multinational teams, they are capable of managing time zones, scheduling meetings, and scheduling appointments.

- These AI technologies save professionals time by managing the tiresome back-and-forth of scheduling, freeing them up to concentrate on more crucial work and save their energy for more strategic thinking.

Effective and productive use of time is ensured by integrating AI tools into individual time management plans. AI gives people control over their schedules, lowering stress and enhancing work-life balance by automating time-consuming chores and offering insights into how time is spent.

8.3 The Value of Human Relationships in an AI Age

It's critical to keep in mind that human connection is still the foundation of both professional and personal success as AI continues to transform the commercial landscape. AI is capable of doing a wide range of tasks quickly and accurately, but it cannot take the place of emotional intelligence, empathy, and interpersonal skills—all of which are essential for both professional and personal success.

Technology and Human Interaction in Balance: We run the risk of ignoring interpersonal interactions and decreasing human engagement the more we depend on AI to do daily activities. AI has the potential to increase efficiency and production, but it must not take the place of genuine communication.

- For instance, companies that solely rely on AI run the risk of losing the human touch that fosters client loyalty, even while AI-driven chatbots can effectively handle customer support concerns.
- Similar to this, using AI only to interact with coworkers in a work environment (for example, by sending automated emails, reports, or suggestions) may result in a lack of engagement and

collaboration. In order to promote teamwork, creativity, and invention, in-person meetings and interactions are still essential.

Preserving Emotional Intelligence in an AI-Powered World: AI lacks emotional intelligence, which is essential for establishing and preserving relationships, even though it can replicate some features of human interaction. One of the most crucial abilities in both personal and professional contexts is emotional intelligence, which is the capacity to identify, comprehend, and control emotions.

- AI is unable to duplicate the distinctively human qualities of emotional sensitivity and empathy. Companies must make sure that, even as they use AI, they maintain emotional intelligence as a top priority in their relationships with customers and executives.
- The most valued human abilities in a world where AI performs more mundane jobs will be emotional intelligence-related, especially in the areas of customer relationship management, leadership, and dispute resolution.

Promoting Human Connections: One of the difficulties in an AI-driven society is making sure that connections in both the personal and professional spheres are not negatively impacted by an excessive dependence on technology. It takes time and effort to establish human connections, and although AI can help with communication, it cannot take the place of in-depth human-to-human engagement.

- among-person or virtual, regular team meetings or social events support the preservation of trust and camaraderie among teams.
- One-on-one personal check-ins with coworkers or staff members promote a supportive environment and make sure that people feel appreciated in ways that go beyond their output.
- In an AI-driven environment, developing solid relationships requires personalized communication and active listening. Real connection comes from knowing the unique wants and concerns of peers, customers, and employees, even while AI can analyze data and make recommendations.

Using AI to Strengthen, Not Replace, Human

Connection: AI should be viewed as a tool to strengthen human connection, not as a substitute for it. AI, for example, can help with data management, freeing up experts to concentrate on the human elements of their work.

- AI can answer standard customer service questions, allowing human agents to have deeper, more meaningful interactions with customers.
- AI-driven data analytics in leadership can offer insights into customer sentiment or team performance, but human leaders still need to understand and interpret this data with empathy in order to make decisions that are well-informed and meet the needs of their customers or teams.

Prioritizing and maintaining the human aspect is crucial in a world where artificial intelligence is taking over. Businesses that integrate AI with an emphasis on human well-being will be best positioned for long-term success because strong interpersonal interactions, emotional intelligence, and meaningful human connections are irreplaceable.

Success driven by AI shouldn't come at the expense of one's own happiness or interpersonal relationships.

CHAPTER 9

DEVELOPING ADAPTABILITY IN AN AI-POWERED FUTURE

The ability to adapt and prosper in a constantly shifting environment is becoming increasingly important as artificial intelligence (AI) continues to enter many facets of life and business. It is crucial for both individuals and organizations to have resilience, which is the ability to bounce back fast from setbacks and adjust to change. The significance of emotional intelligence, methods for surviving technological change, and the abilities and mentalities required to future-proof employment in an AI-driven society are the main topics of this chapter.

9.1 Building Emotional Intelligence in an AI Environment

The ability to identify, comprehend, and control our own emotions as well as those of others is referred to as emotional intelligence (EI). Developing EI is crucial in a time when AI is having a bigger impact for a number of reasons.

Navigating Change with Empathy: Emotional intelligence enables people to relate to stakeholders, clients, and coworkers who might be feeling scared or uncertain when AI technologies upend established roles and procedures. Fostering a supportive work environment requires this empathy.

- By identifying stress indicators and providing the right kind of support, leaders with high emotional intelligence may effectively guide teams through changes while boosting morale and cooperation.
- Employees might feel appreciated during times of transition by using empathetic communication to allay anxieties about losing their jobs.

Improving Communication Skills: One of the main facets of emotional intelligence is effective communication. In order to continue complex conversations and relationships as AI systems take on more tasks, humans must improve their interpersonal abilities.

- In a world where AI may manage fundamental

communication, abilities like constructive criticism, active listening, and dispute resolution become more and more crucial.
- Leaders that place a high value on emotional intelligence can address team members' worries and promote candid discussion about the implications of AI.

Encouraging Self-Regulation and Adaptability

Self-regulation, or the capacity to control one's emotions and impulses, is another aspect of emotional intelligence. It's critical to remain calm and flexible in the face of swift technological development.
- Strong self-control enables professionals to stay proactive rather than reactive as they negotiate the unknowns and difficulties presented by AI.
- Leaders may cultivate a culture of flexibility and ongoing learning by exhibiting emotional resilience and encouraging their people to follow suit.

A person's capacity to prosper in an AI environment can be greatly increased by investing in emotional intelligence education and training. Since human abilities that promote connection and collaboration must advance along with technology, organizations should give emotional intelligence (EI) top priority in their training initiatives.

9.2 Adapting Well to Technological Development

The quick speed at which AI is developing might make people feel unstable, which can cause resistance and worry. Individuals and organizations can implement a number of tactics to increase resilience and prosper in this setting:

Adopting a Growth Mentality: Resilience in the face of difficulties is encouraged by a growth mindset, which holds that skills and intellect can be acquired with commitment and effort. Adopting this perspective allows people to see failures as chances for development and learning rather than insurmountable barriers.

- People can position themselves as lifelong learners and more easily adjust to the changes brought forth by AI by actively seeking out new experiences and abilities.
- By promoting experimentation and creativity, organizations can help teams develop a growth

mindset by removing the fear of failure.

Maintaining relevance and flexibility in a world where artificial intelligence is continuously changing requires a commitment to lifelong learning. Learning new skills should be a top priority for people, especially those that go well with AI technologies.

- Employees can stay up to date on industry trends and developing technology with the support of professional development programs, workshops, and online courses. Professionals may upskill at their own pace with courses in AI, data analysis, and digital transformation offered by platforms like Coursera and edX.
- Companies can also spend money on training initiatives that support their business objectives, giving staff members the skills they need to thrive in an AI-driven workplace.

Creating a Support System: Strong social ties frequently reinforce resilience. During periods of transition, establishing and preserving a network of encouraging peers, mentors, and coworkers can offer resources and

support.
- Participating in online or in-person professional networks or communities can help people manage the difficulties presented by artificial intelligence by facilitating the sharing of best practices and ideas.
- Employers should encourage a collaborative culture that prioritizes group problem-solving and teamwork so that staff members may help one another during changes.

Stress Management Techniques: Resilience depends on stress management. In order to preserve mental health as AI presents new difficulties, people should give self-care and stress-reduction strategies top priority.
- Exercise, meditation, and mindfulness are among techniques that can help people focus better and manage stress. Overall productivity and well-being can be improved by including relaxation methods and breaks into regular routines.
- Employers can support staff in effectively managing stress by promoting employee wellness initiatives and giving them access to workshops, wellness programs, and mental health resources.

By implementing these tactics, people and organizations can develop resilience, which will help them take advantage of AI's prospects and prosper in the face of swift technological change.

9.3 Investing in Your Career in the AI Age

It is more important than ever for people to prepare for the future of their professions as AI continues to transform industries. Developing the abilities and mentality required to succeed in a world where artificial intelligence is a major factor is known as "future-proofing."

Identifying and Developing In-Demand Skills: The first step to future-proofing one's career is to understand which skills are critical in an AI-driven future. The following abilities are becoming more and more in demand:

1. **Data Literacy:** In a world where artificial intelligence (AI) produces insights and analytics, the capacity to comprehend and analyze data is essential. To make wise decisions with AI-generated data, professionals should hone their data analysis

and visualization skills.

2. **Technical Skills:** Candidates can stand out in the employment market by having knowledge of AI technology, programming languages (such Python or R), and machine learning concepts. Professionals can better grasp how to use these tools by learning the fundamentals of AI.

3. **Soft skills,** such as creativity, critical thinking, and emotional intelligence, are just as crucial as technical skills. These abilities allow people to create, adjust to change, and work well in groups that use AI technologies.

Adjusting to New Roles and Responsibilities: The nature of work is changing as regular jobs are automated by AI. Professionals should be prepared for the possibility that integrating AI will lead to changes in jobs and responsibilities.

- Taking on more strategic tasks that call for advanced decision-making, creativity, and interpersonal skills areas where human qualities will always be crucial may be one approach to demonstrate this flexibility.
- Companies can promote a culture of flexibility and

creativity by encouraging staff members to investigate new positions that make use of AI and fit with their interests and strong points.

Lifelong Learning and Professional Development: In an AI-driven environment, a dedication to lifelong learning is essential for job longevity. This commitment entails looking for chances to improve one's skills and continue learning.

- Regular training, conference attendance, and participation in professional forums can all help people stay up to date on the most recent advancements in artificial intelligence and related subjects.
- Seeking advice on skill development and new opportunities from industry leaders can also yield insightful information on navigating career choices in a changing environment.

Networking and Personal Brand Building: Future-proofing a career requires both developing a strong professional network and creating a personal brand. Making connections with organizations, thought leaders, and colleagues in the field can open doors to cooperation and progress.

- Professionals can position themselves as informed contributors in their field by sharing their accomplishments, publications, and ideas on sites like LinkedIn. Having a great internet presence increases exposure and creates new chances.
- Participating actively in industry-specific organizations, webinars, and community events enables people to meet people with similar interests and objectives, promoting cooperation and knowledge exchange.

Developing emotional intelligence, accepting change, and making a commitment to lifelong learning and personal growth are all necessary for creating resilience in an AI-driven future. People may confidently traverse the intricacies of an AI landscape and secure their success in a constantly changing world by using techniques that improve flexibility and future-proof professions.

CHAPTER 10

USING AI TO YOUR ADVANTAGE FOR WEALTH

In a time when artificial intelligence (AI) has evolved from a specialized technology to a vital force for advancement, knowing how to take use of its potential can be crucial to success on both a personal and professional level. This chapter presents methods for using AI as an ally, highlighting how it may be used to accomplish long-term objectives, encouraging creativity and innovation, and offering a workable integration roadmap for daily living and corporate operations.

10.1 Using AI to Advance Your Long-Term Objectives

AI has the potential to be a very effective tool for accomplishing long-term goals. Businesses and people can maximize their chances of success by comprehending and effectively utilizing AI technologies.

Setting specific, quantifiable goals is the first step in leveraging AI to achieve your long-term aims. These objectives can be separated into:

1. **Short-term Goals:** These should be centered on short-term results that support longer-term objectives, including improving customer satisfaction or efficiency.
2. The creation of additional product lines, revenue growth, and market expansion are examples of broader aspirations.

Choosing the Right AI Tools: It's crucial to pick AI tools that complement your unique objectives. Depending on your goals, you might think about:

1. **Data Analytics Tools:** These can assist in seeing patterns and guiding decision-making, allowing companies to successfully modify their plans.
2. **Automation Solutions:** By using AI to automate repetitive operations, teams and individuals can focus on strategic goals while freeing up important resources.
3. **Customer Relationship Management (CRM) Systems:** AI-driven CRMs can offer tailored

insights on customers, increasing their loyalty and level of involvement.

Monitoring and Adapting Strategies: AI can help with real-time data analysis, which enables ongoing evaluation of goals' progress. Key performance indicators (KPIs) should be set up by businesses to gauge success and use AI data to make proactive strategy adjustments.

- **Feedback Loops:** By including feedback systems, teams can gather information about how well AI methods are working, which helps them adjust as needed and adapt to changing market conditions.

Individuals and organizations can promote ongoing development and steady growth by leveraging AI to assist both short-term and long-term objectives.

10.2 AI as a Spark for Creativity and Innovation

Beyond optimization, artificial intelligence (AI) has the potential to be a potent stimulant of creativity and innovation. By embracing AI's potential, people and organizations may create innovative solutions and open up new avenues for thought.

Improving Creative Processes: AI can enhance human creativity by offering resources that make design, content creation, and brainstorming easier. For instance:
1. **Generative AI:** Programs such as OpenAI's GPT-3 can help authors by coming up with ideas for material or by drafting text, freeing up creators to concentrate on improving and polishing their work.
2. **Design Tools:** AI-powered systems may make design suggestions, automate tedious design work, and spot patterns to generate fresh ideas.

Data-Driven Insights: AI's capacity to examine enormous volumes of data yields insights that can guide creative tactics and new product creation. Companies can use leverage:
1. **Customer Insights:** By examining consumer behavior and preferences, businesses can customize goods and services to better satisfy consumer needs.
2. **Market Trends:** Artificial intelligence (AI) systems can go through data to find new trends, giving businesses a competitive edge in predicting client

demands.

Collaborative Innovation: By bringing people together from different fields and geographical locations, AI can promote collaboration. AI-driven project management systems are one example of a tool that can improve teamwork by enabling teams to:

1. **Share Knowledge:** By facilitating the exchange of resources and ideas, collaborative platforms create an atmosphere that might lead to creative solutions.
2. **Hold Virtual Brainstorming Sessions:** AI may help arrange and combine input from various groups, resulting in more thorough and creative answers.

Individuals and organizations can open up new possibilities for development and innovation and establish themselves as industry leaders by adopting AI as a collaborator in the creative process.

10.3 A Guide to AI-Powered Personal and Business Success

An organized strategy is necessary to successfully

incorporate AI into both personal and professional undertakings. This roadmap provides doable actions for utilizing AI to achieve long-term contentment and success.

Step 1: Evaluate Your Goals and Needs

Start by assessing your career and personal objectives. Determine the areas in which artificial intelligence (AI) can be useful, whether it be through better decision-making, higher creativity, or increased efficiency.

Step 2: Investigate AI Technologies and Tools

Examine the available AI solutions that meet your needs. Take into account elements like scalability, simplicity of integration, and the capacity to deliver useful insights. Important things to think about are:

1. **Cost-Effectiveness:** Examine the possible ROI for different AI solutions to make sure the instruments selected will be beneficial.
2. To reduce the learning curve for both you and your team, give priority to technologies that are simple to use and intuitive.

Step 3: is to implement gradually.

Before implementing AI solutions more widely, start by piloting them in particular domains. This makes it possible to identify problems and make changes without using excessive amounts of resources. Track the results and get input to improve the strategy.

Step 4: Encourage an Adaptive Culture

Promote an attitude that welcomes innovation and change. This can be accomplished by:

1. **Development and Training:** Spend money on training courses to give team members the know-how to use AI products efficiently.
2. **Free Exchange of Information:** To create a positive atmosphere, keep the discussion about integrating AI open, soliciting comments and resolving issues.

Step 5: Evaluate and Improve

To assess the effectiveness of AI projects, set up KPIs. Review performance data on a regular basis and alter tactics as necessary. Celebrate successes to inspire more creativity and expansion.

Step 6: Keep Up with AI Developments

Stay up to date on best practices and developments in AI technology. You can stay on the cutting edge of innovation and expand your expertise by participating in webinars, industry forums, and continuing education initiatives.

Individuals and companies may successfully use AI to boost productivity, encourage creativity, and propel long-term growth by adhering to this blueprint.

Transforming AI into a useful ally for prosperity necessitates a strategic strategy that supports innovation, is in line with long-term objectives, and adheres to a well-defined integration roadmap. By utilizing AI's potential, people and organizations can improve their efficacy and efficiency while also opening up new avenues for development, innovation, and fulfillment in a world that is becoming more and more digital.

ABOUT THE AUTHOR

Author and thought leader in the IT field Taylor Royce is well known. He has a two-decade career and is an expert at tech trend analysis and forecasting, which enables a wide audience to understand complicated concepts.

Royce's considerable involvement in the IT industry stemmed from his passion with technology, which he developed during his computer science studies. He has extensive knowledge of the industry because of his experience in both software development and strategic consulting.

Known for his research and lucidity, he has written multiple best-selling books and contributed to esteemed tech periodicals. Translations of Royce's books throughout the world demonstrate his impact.

Royce is a well-known authority on emerging technologies and their effects on society, frequently requested as a speaker at international conferences and as a guest on tech podcasts. He promotes the development of ethical technology, emphasizing problems like data privacy and the digital divide.

In addition, with a focus on sustainable industry growth, Royce mentors upcoming tech experts and supports IT education projects. Taylor Royce is well known for his ability to combine analytical thinking with technical know-how. He sees a time when technology will ethically benefit humanity.

www.ingramcontent.com/pod-product-compliance
Lightning Source LLC
Chambersburg PA
CBHW050312230526
45471CB00005B/2139